J. PAUL
GETTY
Oil Billionaire

J. PAUL
GETTY
Oil Billionaire

By

Bruce S. Glassman

THE AMERICAN DREAM

SILVER BURDETT PRESS
ENGLEWOOD CLIFFS, NEW JERSEY

Designed and produced by Blackbirch Graphics, Inc.

Project Editor: Nancy Furstinger

Manufactured in the United States of America

(Lib. ed.)   10   9   8   7   6   5   4   3   2   1

(Paper ed.)   10   9   8   7   6   5   4   3   2   1

Library of Congress Cataloging-in-Publication Data

Glassman, Bruce.
  J. Paul Getty: oil billionaire/by Bruce Glassman.
    (The American Dream)
  Bibliography: p. 108
  Includes index.
  Summary: Examines the life and career of the business tycoon and oilman who dominated one of the largest business empires ever built by a single man and died owning close to one billion dollars.
    1. Getty, J. Paul (Jean Paul), 1892-1976—Juvenile literature.
  2. Millionaires—United States—Biography—Juvenile literature.
  3. Businessmen—United States—Biography—Juvenile literature.
  4. Petroleum industry and trade—United States—History—Juvenile literature.   [1. Getty, J. Paul (Jean Paul), 1892-1976.
  2.   Businessmen.   3. Millionaires.] I. Title. II. Series: American dream (Englewood Cliffs, N.J.)
  HD9570.G4G57   1989
  332'.092'4—dc19
  [B]   88-8492
  [92]   CIP
                                                                                    AC

ISBN 0-382-09584-7 (lib. bdg.)
ISBN 0-382-09592-8 (pbk.)

Contents

"I have no complex about wealth. I have worked
hard for my money, producing things people need.
I believe that the able industrial leader who creates
wealth and employment is more worthy of
historical notice than politicians or soldiers."
—J. Paul Getty

Introduction

*P*eople around the world seem to have a limitless fascination with those who have acquired great wealth. Because the acquisition of wealth is so widely revered, people want to know what someone with unlimited resources chooses to do with his or her life. And, inevitably, they also enjoy speculating about what they would do with that wealth if it ever came their way. Of all the assumptions people have about the rich, perhaps the two most common are that people's fortunes fundamentally change their nature and that bottomless bank accounts usually serve to liberate and enlighten the people who control them.

In many cases, these assumptions prove to be partially, if not totally, well-founded. Certainly the fortunes of Andrew Carnegie, John D. Rockefeller, and Henry Ford, to name just a few, enabled each of those men to make a lasting contribution to the betterment of our world through various endowments and institutions. The benevolent efforts of those men have been felt long after their personalities have faded, however friendly or disagreeable they might have been. But J. Paul Getty proved to have been one billionaire who stood alone. The wealth he acquired during his lifetime did very little to change him from the man he would have likely become without his money. For many people, that was one of Getty's most disappointing qualities.

To many of us, and to the people who knew him, the personality of J. Paul Getty will not make complete sense. In fact, the contradictions he embodied formed the core of his character. He was a man who would often lie about his family heritage. For example, he once claimed that his family had founded Gettysburg, Pennsylvania. In fact, Gettysburg was founded by a family named Gettys, who were in no way related to the Getty family. Why would one of the richest, most powerful men in the world feel the need to embellish his status by lying about his ancestors? For that matter, why would a man who entered into three failed marriages in five years continue to seek more wives, ultimately marrying twice more? And why did the father who professed to love his youngest son Timmy more than any of his other sons stay in Europe while his child lay dying in a Los Angeles hospital?

Getty was a vain man, obsessed with proving his masculinity and his physical attractiveness to women. But he was also a physical coward—afraid to fly and later to sail. He was the same man who, though he tried to leave his business behind him a number of times, would remain in sole control of his oil empire for forty-six years, longer than any other comparable American businessman in the twentieth century. He was also the man who declared the deepest love and attachment to his disabled mother while at the same time cheating her out of large sums of money.

These contradictions, however, did not stop J. Paul Getty from being one of the greatest and shrewdest business minds in American history. His story tells of a young man who learned to speak more than five languages and who, by sheer virtue of his wits, tenacity, and competitive spirit, made his first million dollars in less than two years at the age of twenty-four. And it tells of one of the largest business empires ever built by a single man, one that dominated the massive oil industry and affected the economy on a global scale.

Perhaps what is most fascinating is that the man who was responsible for these accomplishments had in fact two faces. Privately, he was Getty the loyal son, difficult husband, cold father, passionate lover, liar, cheat, miser, wife-beater, and bigamist. Publicly, he was simply the richest man in the world.

Sarah Risher Getty,
Getty's mother, in 1899,
seven years after his
birth.

Chapter 1

The Young Getty

"Set another place for
lunch."
—*George F. Getty upon
hearing his son's first wail*

*I*n 1890 George and Sarah Getty lost their ten-year-old daughter, Gertrude Lois, to typhoid fever. Sarah also contracted the disease but somehow managed to survive, although partial deafness and minor paralysis would handicap her for the rest of her life.

Still not fully recovered from the loss of her daughter, Sarah became pregnant again two years later and, at the age of forty, gave birth to Jean Paul on December 15, 1892. Neither parent, however, was prepared for the child's arrival.

Where Jean's first name originated is not certain. It does not appear the obvious choice for Scottish-Irish immigrants, for Jean was traditionally considered to be a Scottish girl's name. Perhaps he was named after his father's cousin and law partner, John Getty—a tall, athletic man who apparently long captivated Jean's mother. Sarah and John's relationship was never fully revealed, and their attachment remains a matter for speculation. However, when John committed suicide, it is a fact that Sarah became severely disturbed and emotionally incoherent for a number of weeks.

Sarah's early years with her baby in Minneapolis, Minnesota, were marked by intense overprotectiveness. Determined not to let her second child die, she became possessive and rigid in her child rearing. Yet with all her worrying, she never gave her young son any physical affection. He never had a birthday party or a Christmas tree. And, though he was firmly controlled and constantly watched by his mother, they spent very little real time together. Many have speculated that Sarah's coldness toward her son grew out of her fear of becoming attached. She had lost one child after ten years of complete devotion and the pain of losing another would have been too much for her to bear. For this reason, perhaps, she fulfilled her motherly duties with responsibility but without overwhelming tenderness.

An unemotional, almost frosty, attitude was a quality for which J. Paul Getty would be well known in his later years. It characterized his business style and became the key to his representation in the press. It also kept his family members at a distance from him for his entire life.

J. Paul's father was a stolid man and quite similar to Sarah in his attitude toward rearing young Getty. A well-established Minneapolis insurance lawyer with an impeccable reputation, George Getty was raised in a strict, puritanical atmosphere. As a devout Methodist, he emphatically rejected alcohol, tobacco, dancing, and the theater (all of which his son would embrace, often to excess, in later years). His religious beliefs also influenced his code of ethics; and when it came to business George Getty was known as a pillar of honesty and morality (two virtues that would not guide his son's conduct).

Above: *Getty with his parents and cousin June Hamilton in 1908.*

Below: *Getty (third row, center) with his primary school class in 1906.*

George and Sarah's early years together were marked by relative happiness. When they met in the late 1870s at a small Methodist university established for poor students in Ada, Ohio, they shared a firm belief in well-defined ethics and rigidly honest values.

Both George and Sarah were descended from American immigrant families. Like their ancestors, they were both fiercely independent, strong-willed, and determined to succeed. George was Scottish-Irish and descended from a Presbyterian family that had emigrated in the late 1700s from Londonderry in the north of Ireland. Sarah's Scottish ancestors were part of the McPherson clan and had come to America early in the nineteenth century.

John Getty, George's grandfather, had settled in Maryland in 1790 and became a tavern owner. He was known as a lonely, sour old Irish gentleman who did not get on well with his pioneer neighbors. He froze to death after falling off his horse one night while in a drunken stupor.

When George's father died of diphtheria in 1861, he left his six-year-old son only the prospects of errand work for survival. It was during these formative years that George became obsessed with a hatred of being poor. He drove himself with great determination, allowing himself only a few hours a day for rest and school work. His other hours were spent doing odd jobs and scheming various ways to make a few dollars. His obsession with success and survival would fuel his nearly ceaseless efforts to avoid poverty as he grew up. Even as a successful oil millionaire, George Getty rarely took a day off and almost never let any business dealings take place without his meticulous supervision.

After their marriage on October 30, 1879, the Gettys traveled to Michigan, where George enrolled as a law student. After a few years in Michigan, they moved to Minnesota, where George quickly became the chief lawyer and director of the Northwestern

National Life Insurance company. His solid success and financial accomplishments enabled him to lay down firm roots in the Minneapolis community.

From what is known of their relationship, George and Sarah appear to have been happily married until J. Paul was four years old. At that time his father contracted typhoid and nearly died. For some reason, his illness caused him to renounce his Methodist beliefs and to become a Christian Scientist. George's conversion caused a rift in his marriage and began a period of increasing alienation from his wife. He moved to a second residence in downtown Minneapolis and began to spend more and more time away on business. The separation between his parents was not lost on young Paul. He later wrote to his father that he knew his parents had wanted to divorce at that time.

By 1900, though, George Getty was the forty-five-year-old father of an eight-year-old son, with a wife, an impressive house, and a substantial bank account. It appeared that he was quite content with his position. He was a well-respected business leader in the Minneapolis community and had developed an impressive network of friends and associates. And he had attained the security and success for which he had always yearned. However, in 1903 something happened that made all those accomplishments seem a relatively insignificant part of his life. A bad loan of $2,500, owed to George Getty's company, took him to Oklahoma and changed the lives of the Getty family.

At the turn of the century, Oklahoma was primarily inhabited by Indians. It had been set aside as Indian Territory in 1834 for the Five Civilized Tribes—the Cherokee, Chickasaw, Choctaw, Seminole, and Creek—since westward expansion had pushed the Indians out of their original tribal lands in the southeastern United States.

Coal discoveries in the Choctaw Territories brought the first major influx of white men and

George Getty, photographed in Oklahoma where he earned money as a "wildcatter."

women into Oklahoma in 1870 and spurred the first period of major settlement in the state. By 1897 commercial oil production had begun in Bartlesville and soon spread southward to Tulsa with the discovery of the rich oil reserves of Glenn Pool in the Indian Territory in 1905.

By 1902, just before George Getty arrived, the northern part of the state was already staked out by oil "wildcatters" who hoped to strike it rich by pitching their tents in the wilderness, claiming an area of land, and drilling wells for oil. Wildcatters, oilmen, and criminals populated most of the state's "boom towns" like Bartlesville, where residents gathered to share information and to enjoy the saloons and gambling halls.

These determined individuals were seeking the oil that the Indians in Oklahoma had known about for decades. The Indians, who used oil as a magical cure for an array of physical and emotional ailments, had found it mostly in rock fissures and other natural outlets. Although people had been drilling in Bartlesville since 1870, it was not until the first gusher blew out at Nellie Johnstone's farm, in 1897, that Oklahoma began its phase as a major oil-producing area.

After oil was struck in a number of different locations, the state became flooded with thousands of people who were eager to stake their claim. Wave upon wave of rugged pioneers poured into the Bartlesville area and transformed it into a hotbed of "oil fever." With this massive influx of residents came the need to feed and house the swelling population. Barber shops, post offices, and banks sprang up almost overnight to accommodate a growing demand for services. These "instant cities" also supported a great variety of saloons, gambling houses, and brothels for Bartlesville's ever-growing population.

George Getty traveled to Bartlesville only as a last resort to try to collect the money owed his office.

He found a town populated mostly by Indians, pep-
pered with a steady influx of opportunistic fortune
seekers, prostitutes, and gamblers.

The town, of course, was not the ideal setting for
a man of George Getty's prudence and religious
beliefs. Bartlesville consumed more than $150,000
worth of liquor each year and housed some of the
country's most dangerous outlaws. But the nervous
anticipation of suddenly striking it rich captured
everyone's imagination, including George Getty's.
He quickly began looking into various properties in
the Bartlesville area, trying eagerly to learn as much
about the oil business as he could.

It is not known whether the bad loan was ever
collected. What is known is that Bartlesville in 1903
witnessed one Minnesota lawyer transformed nearly
overnight into an Oklahoma oilman.

The search for oil in the early 1900s embodied
the very character of the "American Dream." Oil was
mysteriously hidden and surprisingly elusive. It was
dangerous, costly, and extremely time-consuming to
locate. In addition, it took wits and cunning to out-
think the scores of searchers hoping to beat the

odds. It took years of sacrifice and patience, and nothing was ever guaranteed. But the potential pay-off was so great that it made any hardship seem endurable.

The quest for oil was also the quest for America's progress. In 1903 signs were everywhere that oil would soon become one of America's most important commodities. Ransom E. Olds was already nearing a production total of five thousand for his one-cylinder automobile known as the Oldsmobile. Orville and Wilbur Wright successfully took to the air for the first time; and a sharp young businessman from Detroit, named Henry Ford, founded a motorcar company. Oklahoma's rapidly growing host of oil millionaires proved that *anything* was possible. It seemed that nothing would stop a hard-working American with a bit of ingenuity from becoming a wealthy tycoon.

Teddy Roosevelt, the youngest man ever to serve as president of the United States, also embod-

Getty oil well workers at the Kern River oil field.

ied the brave and adventurous spirit of America at the turn of the century. A robust and athletic straight talker, Roosevelt inspired the country to strive for economic growth and progress. He convinced Americans that determination and guts could enable any citizen to become successful.

America was buzzing with anticipation. Oil, and all that it could help people accomplish, made Americans giddy with dreams of prosperity. The invention of the mass-produced automobile would soon open up enormous new vistas for the average family. This new mobility would enable people to travel farther and to "expand their horizons" in a very literal as well as figurative sense. New machines that could accomplish unheard of tasks for people were developed at an astounding rate. Soon America would be working faster, more uniformly, and more economically than ever before.

It was during this time that George Getty purchased 1,100 acres in the territory of the Osage Nation, west of Bartlesville, for $500. After a year of searching and drilling, George Getty's first well "blew out." With his newest and most promising prospects a few miles west of Bartlesville, George brought his wife and son to Oklahoma from Minnesota. There he began to build the business that would soon be the cornerstone of the Getty family fortune.

Chapter 2

Son of a Millionaire

"Fine day. Papa gave me
a quarter to put in my
purse."
—*From J. Paul's diary, at
age ten*

Young J. Paul made his first investment at the age of eleven. He bought one hundred shares in his father's Minnehoma Oil Company, a name that combined the family's former home state with that of their new one. In his autobiography, *My Life and Fortunes*, Getty recalls his father's reaction: "Now you're part owner of the company for which I work. You're one of my bosses." It was those words that ushered in the beginning of Minnehoma's great success and the first of many father-son business partnerships. But those words signaled something more. They launched the career of J. Paul Getty, business tycoon and oilman such as the world had never seen.

By the time J. Paul was fourteen, his father had become obsessed with multiplying his newfound fortune and with immersing himself in the business of Minnehoma. The young Getty often found him-

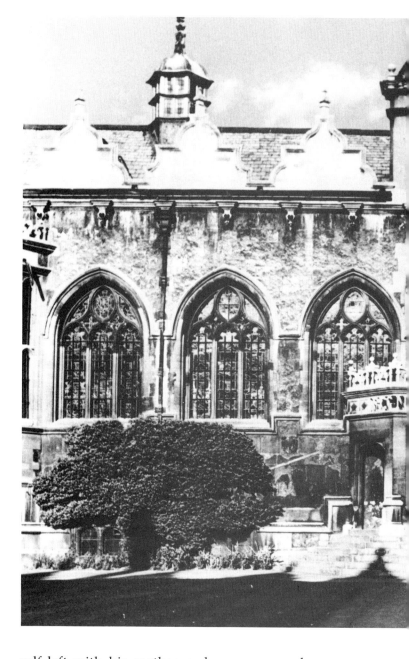

self left with his mother, a dour woman who was now completely deaf, and with whom communication was often a strain. In addition, Sarah's frequent discontent at being left alone by her husband manifested itself in her overpossessive and domineering treatment of her only child. Getty's constant companion during those days—the only creature for whom he ever showed any outward affection—was his mongrel dog named Jip. It was J. Paul's basic

Oriel College, Oxford University, where Getty studied briefly.

feeling of loneliness and his emotional deprivation during these early teenage years that most likely contributed to the "lone wolf" character he developed later in life.

J. Paul was not an easy child to contend with by any standards. He was stubborn and defiant and often displayed a hefty temper. Even though he was obviously intelligent, he refused to apply himself to his studies and nearly failed all his courses in school.

23

Consequently, J. Paul had transferred from various schools in both Minnesota and Oklahoma.

The young Getty was learning quickly that, as the son of an eminent millionaire, very little more than money was needed for success in the world.

By 1907 J. Paul was fifteen and living with his mother in the expensive Tudor mansion his father had purchased the previous year in an up-and-coming California neighborhood called South Kingsley, in Los Angeles. There J. Paul lived in rooms hung with velvet, while he was served by a Japanese cook, a gardener who maintained the spacious grounds, and a chauffeur in charge of several large limousines.

He would write home to his parents telling them he was taking various courses that, in fact, he wasn't.

J. Paul had always known a comfortable life, but the newly acquired Getty wealth propelled the family into a different category of affluence—and one to which J. Paul had no trouble getting accustomed. And it all happened so fast. It had taken George Getty only three years to become one of the biggest independent oilmen in Oklahoma.

Around 1911 J. Paul enrolled at the University of Southern California, but soon transferred to the University of California at Berkeley. In 1912 he took seven academic courses and nearly failed every one. He would write home to his parents telling them he was taking various courses that, in fact, he wasn't. He never studied and would play skillfully on their emotions, making up stories about piano practice and new books in order to get money from home.

Bored with an academic environment, J. Paul decided to take a trip to the Far East. He left from California and was abroad for more than two months. Though his original intention was purely to seek an exotic diversion from the responsibilities of college, his trip proved to be a valuable educational experience. It was during these travels, particularly in Japan, that he became impressed with the industriousness of the Japanese and the beauty of Oriental artwork. He especially admired the Japanese attitude toward work, and most likely admired the complete and utter loyalty displayed by employees toward both the company and the company's bosses.

Getty's return to America only proved to be an opportunity for more academic failings. Tired of university life in America, Getty arranged a transfer to Oxford University in England, as a student unattached to any particular college. Oxford held an allure for him for a number of reasons, not the least of which was its distance from California and Oklahoma.

While attending Oxford, Getty continued to separate himself from his parents, both geographically and emotionally. George seriously began to doubt J. Paul's professed dedication to academics and quickly lost hope of his son ever taking up anything respectable. At the same time, J. Paul felt the need to sever ties with his parents and to become more independent. Driven by a desire to be completely free of responsibilities, he left Oxford and began a leisurely and unstructured journey through Europe. (Though it is uncertain how he completed the requirements, J. Paul Getty is on record at Oxford as the recipient of a degree.)

By 1913 Getty was roaming the French and German countryside in a secondhand Mercedes-Benz, never staying anyplace for more than a few nights. He never left a telephone number or an address; and never informed his parents of his whereabouts or his plans for the future.

During this period J. Paul's father was becoming increasingly annoyed, not only with his son's freewheeling life, but also with J. Paul's insistence that his father support it. Even though he sent $175 each month (a substantial sum in 1913), George was constantly receiving telegrams from J. Paul complaining that he lacked the funds to support the kind of life to which he felt he was entitled. Tensions grew as J. Paul wrote a series of accusatory letters in which he berated his father for holding back the funds that were part of his "birthright." This tactic, however, proved to be a serious mistake. The younger Getty had perhaps lost sight of the fact that he was dealing more with a shrewd, tough-minded businessman than with a loving father. George felt attacked and, as an act of punishment, decided to teach his arrogant heir something of a lesson.

To prompt some action, George wrote to J. Paul and informed him that he had seized his shares of stock in the Minnehoma Oil Company, which had now grown to fifteen thousand. George had commissioned a sports car built for his son a few years earlier in California and he explained that all the shares were eaten up by expenses for the automobile. Ironically (but most likely not by accident), this letter arrived just weeks before J. Paul's twenty-first birthday—the birthday that would bring with it legal as well as financial independence. Instead, upon coming of age, J. Paul lost his only investment.

J. Paul did not take his father's actions lightly. In response, he wrote another letter attacking his father and the unannounced punishment. In the letter to his father, J. Paul explained that the dividends from his shares in the company more than covered the expense of the sports car. In addition, he demanded his shares, his two cars, and $450 in cash from his father immediately. He concluded the letter by saying "your express attitude leaves me no choice. No choice but to deal with the matter as though I were dealing with an opponent." This tone, and this stance, characterized the relationship between the father and son during the following years. It also set a strict precedent for the workings of the family business and foreshadowed the unyielding way J. Paul Getty would later force his own family to become some of his fiercest adversaries.

In June 1914, George and Sarah traveled to Europe in hopes of seeing their son. The trip had been postponed earlier because of a serious lapse in Sarah's health. She apparently suffered a breakdown following the suicide of George's cousin, John Getty, and took months to recover. Now Sarah was anxious to see her child after a year's separation, and George wrote to J. Paul requesting that they meet in Hamburg. George and Sarah never received a response and, on arriving in the German city, were not met by their son.

The Gettys were finally reunited just as Europe began to rumble with the aftermath of the assassination of Austrian Archduke Francis Ferdinand, which led to World War I. J. Paul managed to catch up with his parents in Paris in 1914 and to convince them that he was homesick. As soon as the situation in Europe became serious and threatening, J. Paul decided that travel had lost its appeal and it was time to return to the United States. He sailed with his parents on the *Lusitania*. Just a year later, the ship was torpedoed by the Germans off the Irish coast, killing 1,198 people and forcing the United States to enter the war.

As J. Paul returned to America, his thoughts turned back to oil and money-making. He also was determined to retrieve the stocks his father had unjustly seized. With these goals in mind, J. Paul agreed to try his hand at the oil business in a partnership with his father. George must have been pleased at the prospect of his only son, not only undertaking a "respectable career," but joining the family business as well. J. Paul agreed to seek out and evaluate potentially lucrative oil properties in Oklahoma. The elder Getty agreed to advance him $100 a month and promised to provide investment capital for financing the purchase of promising real estate. Any profits would be split 70/30, with the majority going to Getty senior. George asked only that his son stick with the business for a year. If things didn't work out, he explained, or if J. Paul did not like his position, he was free to leave. Accepting the challenge, J. Paul took off for Tulsa with his father, eager to make a success of his new career.

Getty, at age 44, was already one of the richest men in America.

Chapter 3

Shrewd Young Oilman

"I will stay in Tulsa
until I make a million
dollars."
—*J. Paul Getty in 1915,*
after his first year's profit
of $40,000

*J*ust as his father had stepped into the seedy world of Bartlesville a decade earlier, J. Paul Getty arrived in Tulsa, Oklahoma, in 1914 ready to make his fortune. At the age of twenty-two, he found himself surrounded by the same relentless opportunists and outcasts that had come to characterize almost every boom town in America. It was a fast, dirty, ruthless, and greedy world in which most people carried rifles either to protect their interests or to settle scores. J. Paul Getty, on the other hand, was known as the only man in Tulsa to wear a wristwatch and, while others were trying to make their money by cheating or strong-arming the defenseless, he armed himself with a detailed knowledge of the oil industry and an unyielding seriousness toward his business.

In a magazine interview many years later, Getty admitted that during his first year "fortune eluded" him. He was, after all, just a kid, new to a business that had defeated men twice his age with years of experience. But he quickly learned how to spot potential properties and soon began to play by the established rules, which did not value honesty or charity very highly.

Getty decided to travel south of Tulsa in search of property and soon purchased a half interest in the lease of the Nancy Taylor farm in Stonebluff. His purchase, which entitled him to a percentage of any profits if oil was struck, went against the conventional wisdom of the other oilmen in the area and caused him, on a few occasions, to be the butt of jokes concerning his business skills. The jokes ended, however, when oil was found on the Taylor farm and young Getty made the first killing of his oil career. Later he recalled: "A lot of people thought there was no oil there; and even more people tried to persuade me that I was in the wrong place to drill. But I was stubborn and not about to be moved. It paid off."

Three days after he had struck oil, Getty sold the lease to a big Tulsa oil company and split the profit 70/30 with his father. J. Paul's share came to $11,850—his first profit from an oil deal. It also meant his father could formally accept him into the family business.

J. Paul was soon made director of Minnehoma— his father's master company, which owned leases west of Bartlesville (where 17 percent of America's oil was produced in 1916). Minnehoma produced a few hundred barrels of oil each day there and was worth between one and two million dollars.

A number of factors enabled J. Paul to witness a great increase in profits in the years that followed. Between 1903 and 1916, oil prices fluctuated wildly, along with profits for oil companies. But World War I, fought by mechanized vehicles on the ground and in the air, created a great demand for oil and caused a tremendous increase in its price. This increase, of course, was a great boon to oilmen, who saw the price of oil go from 40 cents a barrel in 1915 to $2.23 a barrel by 1918.

While he continued to purchase successful oil-rich properties near Stonebluff, J. Paul lived at the Cordova Hotel, a popular residence for many of Tulsa's wildcatters. He also spent a great deal of time in the lobby of the Hotel Tulsa, where oilmen gathered to trade information on important strikes or to pick up the latest news on oil prices. It was in this lobby that Getty learned the value of cultivating acquaintances in order to gain access to elite "business circles." Such groups circulated "valuable tips" and could help someone get rich. He also learned that having the right information gave one valuable leverage and influence with competitors.

During this time, Getty concentrated only on the buying and selling of leases. He spent neither time nor money drilling for oil, partly because he did not yet have the resources to tie up in such a speculative endeavor. He would buy leases, however, and, like stocks, would hold onto them until they increased in value. He spent all of his time in areas that had been shunned by other oilmen, for he knew that those were the areas in which the best bargains could be found.

Many of his peers ridiculed him for thinking that some fields near Noble and Garfield, in the middle of the Oklahoma Territory, contained anything worth noticing. But Getty was convinced that there was some logic to nature and to the way oil flowed under the ground. Determined to explore in the less conventional ways, he began to employ some basic principles of geology in order to assess the underground wealth of various areas. Getty was one of the first of a handful of oilmen to use geology as an aid, for most old-time oilmen did not trust such a science. Most still preferred to look for crude oil in streams and in fissures in rock. Few businessmen were convinced that anything could be gained by

*

Getty was one of the first of a handful of oilmen to use geology as an aid.

studying rock formations and surface features of the land.

Emil Kluth, a Swiss geologist originally sent to the United States by a French-backed firm, was the first scientist to be hired by Getty. While most of the other oilmen were ignorant about geology, Getty was different. He had the advantage of some formal education and was not so quick to dismiss something simply because it was new. Getty used Kluth to do some of the early surveys near the Nancy Taylor property and then employed him to work west of the "accepted" oil territory in northern Oklahoma. There he eventually found fields in Garber and Billings. In fact, Kluth turned out to be one of Getty's most valuable employees. With the scientist's help in 1916, Getty went on a lease-buying frenzy and began to drill, buy, and sell property wildly. He then realized after only five months that he was worth more than a million dollars.

Getty found that it was, in his case, a great asset to be independent in the oil business. He had no overhead, and was able to keep every aspect of his costs at a minimum. Most importantly, Getty was able to make decisions quickly without having to answer to anyone else. This independence would continue to be one of his greatest strengths (perhaps *the* greatest), and one that would later enable him to parlay his small fortune into a massive one.

All in all, it had taken George F. Getty thirteen years to make $425,000 from the production of his first oil field in Oklahoma. His son, though he started with more of an advantage, had made his first million before the end of his second year in the business. But J. Paul would not do with his money what one would expect of a budding entrepreneurial genius. Instead of reinvesting his million in hopes of multiplying it, Getty deserted the Oklahoma oil fields and went to California to retire. At twenty-four, much to the dismay of his father, J. Paul decided to use his money to relax and have fun.

But fun would soon prove to have its own head-aches. Returning to the house at South Kingsley in Los Angeles, J. Paul turned his attentions to his social life. Unfortunately, during this time, a local woman named Elsie Eckstrom claimed that while she was visiting Getty, he gave her too much to drink and "took advantage" of her. She then claimed he was the father of her baby. In addition to the serious-ness of her claim, the story became something of a public scandal and gave Getty his first taste of bad publicity. It also humiliated and mortified both Sarah and George.

Though the baby was not born until ten months and three days after the supposed seduction, the newspapers provided full coverage, and the name Paula Getty was recorded on the child's official birth certificate. The entire episode was an obvious at-tempt by Elsie's lawyers to extract money from one of California's youngest millionaires. Getty was sued for $100,000; however, the case was settled out of court for an undisclosed amount.

A bit shaken, and somewhat disillusioned, the young oilman decided to return to the Oklahoma oil fields to resume work with his father. Whether his return was an effort to regain his father's approval, to replenish his bank account after the suit, or simply because he was bored without the challenge of steady work, is not known. What is certain is that the lesson he learned (however small) from the Califor-nia episode would not be enough to prevent him from making even bigger mistakes in the very near future.

La Brea Tarpits, near Getty's home in Los Angeles.

Chapter 4

Irresponsible and Irrepressible

"I realized that I was an eyewitness to the violent death of an era." —*J. Paul Getty referring to the stock market crash of 1929 in his autobiography* My Life and Fortunes

*B*y the 1920s oil, and the gasoline that was made from it, had already made many Americans very rich. California in particular had an abundance of residents who had made their fortunes drilling for the substance that the Spaniards who had inhabited the area as far back as 1769 called *la brea*. Advances in factory production in the first decade of the 1900s (forged to a great degree by auto pioneer Henry Ford) spurred the steady growth of gas-consuming automobiles across the country by making them more accessible as well as more afford-able. The growing popularity of air travel also helped to make the oil-rich state of California a literal gold mine. Nearly one quarter of all the oil produced in the United States was being pumped just hours from the Getty's home in Los Angeles.

The California oil business, unlike that of Okla-homa, was dominated by a few very large and powerful oil companies, such as Standard Oil, Union Oil, and the Southern Pacific Company. Getty's company was still too small to compete seriously with these large concerns. However, since there was still plenty of oil to be had, he began to drill and buy properties near sites where others had struck significant amounts of oil.

In 1921 J. Paul Getty purchased a lease at Telegraph Hill, near Santa Fe Springs, for $693,000. Two years later the hill was overrun with oil derricks, and Getty's lease (shrewdly purchased at the top of the hill's crest where the dome of the oil pool was located) was already worth many times what he had paid for it. Production of oil at Telegraph Hill went from 218,000 barrels in 1921 to 70 million barrels in 1923.

George Getty's new company—George F. Getty, Inc., founded in 1924—was dedicated to developing California oil interests. Telegraph Hill alone would supply $6.4 million to the company in the following fifteen years. It seemed the father-and-son partnership was working with some success, certainly from a financial point of view. But the father and son were, in some respects, an odd combination. George, now sixty-eight, was legendary in the oil business for his honesty; his handshake was highly preferred (by most who knew him) over a written contract. His son, on the other hand, had a reputation as a wily, greedy man who would turn a profit at anyone's expense. George and J. Paul often conflicted on buying strategies and management style but more often than not they managed to leave their respective deals to each other.

In 1923 George Getty suffered a partially paralytic stroke, which put a temporary halt to Getty business as usual. J. Paul felt it was a particularly opportune time to try to seize control of the family company, but his father, speech impaired and paralyzed on one side of his body, ordered his son to stay out of the affairs of the company. During his recuperation in the following months, George Getty ran his oil empire from his sickbed.

Shunned by his father, J. Paul then concentrated his efforts on enhancing his already established reputation in Los Angeles as a lover of beautiful young women and wild parties. He began to date an eighteen-year-old, Jeanette Demont, and subsequently eloped with her in October 1923. Though neither of J. Paul's parents met Jeanette until they had been married for a number of months, they must have been cheered by the fact that their son had apparently settled down. Their first grandson, George II, born July 9, 1924, might have seemed further proof of J. Paul's desire for a more sedate lifestyle.

But J. Paul's apparently more traditional behavior was illusory. He had not settled down at all. In fact, his love for women and parties became even greater after his marriage. Only two months after their wedding, Getty began taking other women to night clubs and indulging in a series of flagrant affairs. He was seen yelling at his wife in public and was known to have threatened her life on a number of occasions. After less than two years of marriage, Jeanette Getty filed for divorce. Her reasons included beatings, bruisings, and being locked in a closet shortly after George II was born. The abuse Jeanette suffered, along with her failed marriage, took a serious toll on her. Eventually, she became a patient in a mental institution, where she would go into shock and hysterics after every visit from her estranged husband. Later, however, she got remarried to a stockbroker named Bill Jones, and young George lived with them.

Getty left California in disgrace in 1926 and journeyed to Mexico and Venezuela in hopes of entering the oil business south of the border. It appeared that J. Paul wanted to impress his parents by opening up the Mexican oil fields for production. It was also his way of asking George and Sarah's

Crowds fill the streets across from the New York Stock Exchange in October 1929. Getty found the crash a valuable financial lesson.

forgiveness for his shameful divorce and embarrassing reputation.

It was during J. Paul's six-month stay in Mexico that he met Allene Ashby and her sister Belene, the teenage daughters of a wealthy Texas rancher. After a brief courtship, J. Paul and Allene eloped in Cuernavaca and were married on October 27, 1926. Technically, this act made Jean Paul Getty a bigamist, for his divorce from Jeanette was not final until the papers came through in September 1927. The fact that Getty was having an affair with Belene while married to Allene also put him in the unique position of being unfaithful to two wives at the same time. Only a few weeks after their wedding, Allene and Getty separated, admitting that their marriage had been a grave mistake.

J. Paul's romantic escapades continued to strain his relationship with his parents. Not only were they ashamed of him and his exploits, but many of his digressions caused well-publicized scandals that exposed the family to worldwide ridicule. By December 1926, George decided that some punitive action was in order. He promptly removed his son from the Minnehoma board and revised his will without his son's knowledge.

J. Paul Getty spent the summer of 1928 in Vienna. There he met a young German teenager named Adolphine Helmle, who had just completed a convent education and was traveling with her parents. Getty took a liking to "Fini" and asked for her hand in marriage. She accepted, though her father— a doctor of engineering and director of the Badenwerk electricity company—was less than overjoyed at the prospect. They were married in Havana, Cuba, in December 1928 and honeymooned in Florida. Fini was Getty's third wife in less than five years.

When Sarah and George's fiftieth wedding anniversary was celebrated in October 1929, J. Paul had to decide whether to attend the gala party for his parents in California or go to Wall Street to study firsthand the recent crash in the stock market. He chose to travel to Wall Street, where he witnessed the terrible consequences of America's financial collapse. His experience there, as he wrote later in his diary, proved to be a valuable one, and one that taught him a great deal about finance, stocks, and the intricate workings of the United States economy.

In the meantime, Fini returned to Germany, pregnant with Getty's second child, Jean Ronald. Only nineteen years old, she had been unhappy often being left alone in her house with Sarah Getty for weeks on end, and without seeing her husband. She did not speak English well and yearned to return to her parents. J. Paul found his way to Germany shortly after Fini's return. After a failed brief reunion with his wife, he received word of his father's second stroke. The prognosis for George was not good. Getty spent the next nine days on trains and boats in order to reach his father's side in Los Angeles.

When J. Paul arrived, he was shocked to find that his father was not being well attended. George had followed his Christian Scientist beliefs and refused any conventional medicine. He was cared for only by Christian Scientist practitioners who left him propped up in bed, without proper nursing. A few days after J. Paul's arrival, on May 31, 1930, George Getty, Oklahoma oil pioneer and one of the richest men in Los Angeles, died.

Throughout his life, Getty was fascinated by glamorous younger women. Here, he dances with an unidentified socialite.

Chapter 5

Mother and Son

"What you're trying to
tell me is that J. Paul is
a crook."
—*Sarah Getty after being
advised that her son was
trying to sell her a useless
oil well in Signal Hill*

*F*or J. Paul Getty, his father's
death came as a great blow, mostly because the bulk
of George's estate (more than $10 million) was left to
Sarah. In addition, control of Getty Oil interests was
left to the executors of the estate—Security-First
National Bank of Los Angeles and H. Paul Grimm, a
long-time associate of George's. J. Paul, at the age of
thirty-eight, was left a total of $500,000, minus
$250,000, which he still owed his father from his
purchase of 33 percent of George F. Getty, Inc., in
1928. Even J. Paul's six-year-old son, George II, faired
better than his father, inheriting $300,000 from his
grandfather.

Getty felt hurt and cheated by the treatment he
had received from his father. Nevertheless, he persisted with the affairs of the family company. On
July 30, 1930, he was elected president of George F.
Getty, Inc., and was left to contend with the consid-
erable power of his major stockholder—his mother.

The new president was full of elaborate plans for the expansion of his company. He dreamed of a fully integrated corporation that could drill, refine, transport, and sell its own oil and gas without falling prey to the big businesses that often squeezed the smaller competitor for storage capacity, pipelines, and access to markets. But Sarah was to pose a great obstacle to J. Paul's grandiose schemes. Conservative and cautious, she would not favor great outlays of capital and risky extensions of credit and assets necessary to realize many of her son's dreams.

Moreover, J. Paul viewed the Great Depression not as a tragedy that had ruined the lives of countless Americans, but rather as a great investment opportunity. He was ready to make his move by acquiring stocks and other investments during a time when most other investors were running scared. Getty had the insight and determination to go against the obvious signs of economic disaster, and he began buying up shares in anything that struck him as a bargain. It was perhaps this single strategy that made the greatest contribution to Getty's financial success during this period.

Though many of his stocks would not immediately show great profits, J. Paul felt, in the 1930s, that he was on to a major new business philosophy. In the 1920s, exploring, drilling, and producing oil made the most sense for the small, independent investor. Oil-company stocks were greatly inflated during those boom years and it was cheaper to buy leases and drill in hopes of tapping into a gusher. But the crash of 1929, and the Depression that followed it, created a dramatic undervaluing of stocks. Willing buyers were now able to purchase shares at a fraction of their worth, relative to the oil they represented in the ground. J. Paul Getty, with available capital and an eagle eye for bargains, was one of the few businessmen to realize the opportunity that existed on Wall Street. Consequently, while other investors were hoarding their money and waiting for the Depression to blow over, Getty was buying up stocks as fast as he could.

Sarah Getty, on the other hand, was opposed to buying common stocks in 1930. On a number of occasions mother and son had violent arguments on the subject, and on more than a few occasions, were overheard by other members of the Getty staff. Eventually, J. Paul convinced enough of the company directors to vote in favor of buying shares in two California oil producers—Pacific Western and Mexican Seaboard. Getty bought $3 million worth of shares with a margin account from E.F. Hutton and a $2.5 million loan from Security-First National Bank. The stock market soon sagged, however, and caused Getty Oil a $1 million "paper loss" (a loss of $1 million in the overall worth of Getty's assets). Security-First then forced Getty to sell off the Mexican Seaboard stock to pay off part of the loan, Sarah offered her usual recriminations, and J. Paul was severely humiliated.

This setback only proved to make J. Paul Getty braver and more confident. He now set his sights on acquiring Pacific Western by using the financial leverage that remained in George F. Getty, Inc. Through a series of shrewd loans, investments, and stock purchases, Getty managed to add Pacific Western to the family businesses. One of his first moves at the new company was to fire all the employees and then hire them back at severely reduced salaries. It was a strategy that could only work during a nationwide Depression, when labor had no choice but to take any jobs that were available.

Getty's next project was more ambitious. He wanted to acquire Tide Water Associated Oil Co.— the ninth largest in the United States, with 1,233 service stations and assets totaling more than $200 million. Tide Water produced crude oil that would be quite a boon to Getty's refineries in Bayonne, New Jersey, and San Francisco, and Getty wanted the company passionately. To raise working capital for

his plan, Getty sold some of his company's valuable land in Kettleman Hills, Oklahoma, to Shell for $4.5 million in cash. The sale enabled him to wait for just the right moment to start making a play for Tide Water.

On March 12, 1930, Swedish match magnate Ivar Kreuger committed suicide in Paris. Then George Eastman, of Eastman Kodak, killed himself in Rochester, New York. Their deaths caused many stock-market officials to panic. When news finally

An Iraqi oil well. In the 1930s Getty tried to invest in Iraqi oil, but the area was opened instead to the larger British Oil Development Company.

leaked to the public, Eastman Kodak shares plummeted and took several other companies down with it.

During all this confusion a modest order to buy Tide Water shares was presented on the floor of the stock exchange by the Los Angeles office of E.F. Hutton, on behalf of an unknown investor. On March 15, Getty's first 1,200 shares went for $2.50 each, almost the lowest point they would ever reach. By the end of the month, Getty had accumulated more than 15,000 shares. "Buy when everyone else is selling and hold on until everyone else is buying" was his credo at the time.

With his acquisition of Tide Water well underway, Getty became interested in expanding his oil interests in the Middle East. His financial resources were stretched to the limit and it is amazing that he would consider any other investing at all. But Getty's business style in the 1930s was nothing less than courageous.

Iraq, in 1930, had become anxious to exploit more of its oil resources and to increase its oil exports and revenues. When Getty heard that drilling rights to the lands west of the Tigris River were to be conceded to the highest bidder, he immediately enlisted a local agent, Albert Kasperkhan, to open negotiations on his behalf. But the competition, which included the Iraq Petroleum Company, proved to be rather stiff. Iraq Petroleum, a gigantic oil conglomerate, comprised major companies such as Gulf, Shell, and Standard Oil, to name only a few.

The U.S. State Department offered to help Getty forge what they called an "open door policy" for oilmen in the Middle East. The United States government arranged for Getty to meet Iraq's prime minister, but personal negotiations were not entirely successful. However, Getty did not give up. He began spreading bogus information about his power and influence in the American government. Not only did he promise to pay very high royalties on oil, but he also guaranteed political aid to Iraq via his friends "from President Hoover on down." After doing a little fact checking, the Iraqi government found that Getty's company was only worth a piddling $30 million and decided it was not big enough to invest in Iraq sufficiently. The concession went to the British Oil Development Company instead.

The failure with Mexican Seaboard and the failure in Iraq were not the only upsets for the oilman in the early 1930s. By November 1930, Fini had initiated Getty's third divorce and J. Paul became obsessed with a twenty-two-year-old woman named Ann Rork. After traveling briefly together, they took a suite of rooms at the Plaza Hotel in New York in August 1931. There they decided to declare themselves married without any of the legal hassle usually required for such a ritual. With Ann eight months pregnant, they boarded a ship bound for Italy in 1932. Before they reached their destination, however, Eugene Paul was born. Three months later they were formally married.

No sooner had they landed in Genoa than Getty left his wife and newborn son to travel to Paris to entertain a number of his female admirers. After Ann had recuperated from childbirth, she rejoined her husband in France but was treated cruelly. He gave her little money for meals, refused to offer any assistance or to hire a nurse for the child, and left almost immediately for America.

Ann was finally reunited with Getty in the United States, but Sarah was not informed of their marriage or her new grandson until a number of months afterward. Getty was completely uninterested in anything having to do with family, but Ann could not manage to stay away from him. "He did not want to hear or smell children," she said of him. "He wanted them for his dynasty but didn't want to deal with them as babies." But her husband's lack of interest did not deter Ann from becoming pregnant again in 1933. As expected, when Getty learned the news, he was off again, this time to Germany for the full nine months of his wife's second pregnancy.

Getty in 1939, shortly after his return from Europe, where he negotiated an oil sale to Russia.

Chapter 6

Taking Control

"Most of the people in top management of American business are promoted clerks, engineers, and salesmen. I like Benjamin Franklin's advice: 'If you want it done correctly, do it yourself.' I do it all myself. How many others are there like me?"
—*J. Paul Getty*

While in Germany, Getty witnessed Hitler's rise to power firsthand. His friends observed a certain admiration in him toward the Nazis, a respect for their utter ruthlessness and impeccable efficiency. Fini would later testify in a divorce proceeding that Getty was friends with many of the highest-ranking officials of the Reich and that, on one occasion, Getty met with Hitler and received a necktie as a present from the Führer. His association with the Nazis, and his frequent visits to Germany in the coming years, would prove to be more destructive to his personal career than the oil-man would ever imagine.

Back home, after Ann had given birth to her second son, Gordon, she found to her surprise that her husband had returned from his travels in Germany. Getty arrived at the hospital three hours after Gordon's birth. But he stayed for only five minutes.

The Getty Museum in Malibu, California cost Getty $10 million to build, and houses much of his personal art collection.

It was now obvious to Ann that marriage would not make J. Paul Getty a family man. In 1934 she and her two boys moved into a rented house in Santa Monica, but Getty would not live with them for any length of time. When he did come home, it was usually late at night and he would verbally abuse Ann without mercy. He tried to hurt her by bragging about his unfaithfulness.

Even with his personal life in shambles, Getty managed to continue planning for a bigger and better oil company. His next priority was to try to gain control of his mother's two-thirds ownership of George F. Getty, Inc., so that he could have complete

power to borrow the money he needed to go after the remaining shares of Tide Water.

Sarah was not an easy adversary. She had been the director of Minnehoma since 1906 and director of George F. Getty, Inc., since it was founded in 1924. She did not let her emotions cloud her business dealings, especially with her son.

In 1933 J. Paul and his mother, the two stockholders, went head-to-head on a number of issues. J. Paul objected to loans made to the George F. Getty Oil Company, a separate company owned entirely by Sarah, which explored various Mexican oil interests. The arguments between mother and son soon

Getty (second from left) appraises a painting from his Malibu museum with an expert from Christie's Auction Rooms in London.

became so severe that the company's chief lawyer quit in frustration. Before he left, however, he advised Sarah—who was now eighty years old, deaf, obese, and unable to walk—to sell out to her son for $1 million.

For some unknown reason, on Christmas day 1933, Sarah felt the time had come to sell. She offered to part with her 67 percent share of George F. Getty, Inc., for $4.5 million. J. Paul, who jumped at the chance, was to pay his mother not with cash, but with interest-bearing promissory notes that yielded 3.5 percent interest and could be cashed over the next several years. In return, Sarah would give her son a Christmas present of $850,000 to pay off his margin debt to E.F. Hutton and another loan obligation to George F. Getty, Inc. She informed her son that her offer would only last until noon on December 30, at which point if no response had been made, the offer would be withdrawn and terminated. It didn't take J. Paul very long to make his decision, however. The offer was quickly accepted and Sarah went from being Getty's largest shareholder to Getty's largest creditor.

Getty's enormous debt of $4.5 million did not put the company in a position to obtain funds from any bank. It soon became apparent to J. Paul that he had to rid the company of this debt in order to regain financial solvency. He still yearned to wrest control of Tide Water, but didn't have a chance if he could not borrow money. He immediately turned his energy to convincing his mother that the purchase of shares in Mission Corporation (a company created by Standard Oil to hold the Tide Water shares) was essential to gaining control of Tide Water. At first, Sarah did not share her son's enthusiasm for controlling Mission Corporation. He then urged his mother to make a gift of the promissory notes (a "gift" that would have canceled the George F. Getty, Inc., debt by eliminating the need to repay the notes) and tried to convince her that she did not need the large annual income of $140,000 from the interest she received. Sarah was not easily convinced, and Getty was characteristically surprised that his mother was not quick to make a gift of $4.5 million. Nevertheless, he continued to plead with his mother and stayed with her, sometimes for days at a time.

Sarah knew her son would eventually get what he wanted. Her primary concern was ensuring the family fortune for future generations and making sure her husband's legacy was not carelessly squandered by her overly ambitious son. Sarah's solution was to create a trust that would protect both Getty and his children while it provided money for expanding the oil company. Two and a half million dollars of the notes from J. Paul went into the trust to ensure against any unfortunate financial condition, including bankruptcy. Sarah asked that Getty contribute $1 million to the trust as well. The rest of the money, as Getty had hoped from the start, was given as a gift.

When the transfer of power was complete, J. Paul Getty was the sole trustee of George F. Getty, Inc. He had absolute power and, through financial sleight of hand and money-leveraging (using the "paper value" of assets to borrow money for investment), Getty was never forced to produce his $1 million cash contribution. He would later proudly confide to an aide: "I just fleeced my mother."

The Sarah Getty Trust soon became the foundation of the Getty empire and was used countless times to back ventures and to provide the resources needed to make the shrewdest moves at the most critical times. The power of the trust, too, would become enormous. Though it was valued at a mere $3.7 million when it was created in 1934, by 1985 it was producing a daily income of more than $1 million a day.

Chapter 7

The Great Expansion

"Be thrifty, save a little money, and leave a small surplus for investment."
—*J. Paul Getty's formula for business success*

*B*y using the stock market to gain control of companies, Getty became one of America's first modern takeover strategists. And, utilizing his techniques, he finally found a way to take control of Tide Water.

After Tide Water's owner, John D. Rockefeller's Standard Oil, was threatened by Getty in an antitrust suit, they formed a holding company called Mission Corporation to hold shares of Tide Water. For a while, this averted any problems the company may have faced. But soon after, Getty found out that Rockefeller's shares in Mission would be up for sale (Rockefeller was trying to rid himself of certain interests for tax purposes). Working fast, Getty purchased Rockefeller's 10 percent share in Mission and continued in hot pursuit of more. It took him all of 1935 and 1936 to acquire 641,000 shares (40 percent)

Getty (left) and Claude H. Rosenstein wait to testify for the defense in Charlie Chaplin's trial on Mann Act charges, 1944.

of Mission. Though it was still not the majority of shares, Getty was now the greatest single stockholder.

By 1937 Getty was using his substantial dividends from Tide Water and Skelly Oil (owned by Tide Water) to buy more shares in Pacific Western and Mission. As his base grew, he increased his wealth by purchasing underpriced shares in companies that controlled valuable, though untapped, oil in the ground.

Getty became obsessed with buying cheap controlling shares in oil reserves and then drilling and developing those sources with his own equipment. These purchases, along with the eventual recovery of the economy (which multiplied the value of his stocks), formed the basis of Getty's expanding fortune throughout the 1930s. By the late 1930s, the stock market's Dow Jones Industrial Average had doubled since 1932, indicating a strong growth in America's businesses, and the automobile industry was beginning to grow at an astounding rate. This growth provided a growing market for Getty's greatest commodity. J. Paul's unrelenting talent for uncovering some of Wall Street's greatest bargains, along with his unique blend of courage and stubbornness, made George F. Getty, Inc., worth more than $27 million by 1940.

But success in the business world did not equip J. Paul Getty for success in his personal life. Divorce proceedings in Los Angeles made public many of the sordid details of Getty's marriage to Ann and created bad publicity about him. In retreat, he fled to New York and took up residence on Sutton Place. As he came into contact with Manhattan's "high society," he attempted to enhance his image by cultivating an interest in fine art—particularly oil paintings and antiques. Not surprisingly, this new passion coincided with a slump in the art market, when many fine pieces were being sold at attractive prices.

As his interest increased, Getty hired private tutors to supplement the knowledge he was absorbing through his intense reading on the subjects. He studied the history of eighteenth-century French craftsmen, the materials they used, and the various techniques of production. He learned everything he could about antiques, rugs, tapestries, and furniture. Getty knew that serious art collecting involved serious expenditures; however, he was not one to spent money without investigating the facts.

The new art collector started pursuing works that had traditionally been ignored by others. These works included busts of Greek and Roman emperors and many objects of decorative art from eighteenth-century France.

One of his greatest coups was an early Rembrandt, a portrait of a wealthy Amsterdam grain merchant, Martin Looten, which Getty purchased in 1938 for $65,000. A decade earlier, a rich Dutch businessman had paid three times that price. Although the Dutch art world was outraged at the sale of the

Getty displayed a newly purchased Rembrandt at the 1939 World's Fair in New York.

Rembrandt and its subsequent removal from Holland, the piece added the crowning touch to Getty's collection and was on display at the World's Fair at Flushing Meadows, New York, in 1939. Getty's art collection, like most of his assets, quickly multiplied in value and increased his wealth.

His time in New York also provided the forty-six-year-old Getty with introductions to a number of interesting women. The most notable of these was twenty-three-year-old Teddy Lynch, a talented young lady with a promising career in opera.

As soon as Getty's final divorce papers arrived from Ann in California, Teddy's mother announced the impending marriage of her daughter to one of the country's richest men. But the actual wedding would not take place immediately. In the meantime, J. Paul Getty had too many deals, and too many women, to look after in other parts of the country.

An opportunity arose in 1938 to purchase the forty-two-story Pierre Hotel at Fifth Avenue and 61st Street, off Central Park in Manhattan. The hotel's profits had been slipping even before the Depression but, since the early 1930s, the loss was increasing. Not one to pass up a bargain of any kind, Getty bought the hotel for $2.35 million, less than 25 percent of the original cost of construction.

His first aim was to make the Pierre Hotel the newest fashionable place for New York's cafe society. To attract the proper clientele, Getty asked Manhattan's most sought-after dinner guest, Rhinelander Stewart, to establish himself in the restaurant. Cafe society followed his lead and the establishment quickly boomed.

While the Pierre Hotel was making a splash in New York, Getty set his sights on obtaining a diplomatic post in the Roosevelt administration. His first maneuver was to enlist the help of a public-relations friend who was a distant relative of the president and who had worked with Eleanor Roosevelt in the 1932 election. After painting an almost saintly picture for

White House aides, who were told Mr. Getty had been divorced only twice instead of four times, an appointment was requested with the president. Not surprisingly, though, no invitation was ever extended.

Getty was, however, screened as a possible applicant for other high-ranking jobs. However, interviewers who noted certain associations with the Nazis and some bad publicity from Los Angeles maintained strong reservations about the candidate's profile. Although he persisted with his requests, the ultimate decision from the White House on Getty was negative.

Despite his apparent failure with Roosevelt's people, Getty hired some powerful lawyers and enlisted the help of William McAdoo, a powerful California senator, to lobby the president for a post as United States Ambassador to Russia. Getty made a substantial donation to McAdoo's reelection campaign. Although Roosevelt granted his colleague from California serious consideration, he decided he would not be railroaded into accepting a man of Getty's rather dubious reputation into his administration.

Roosevelt's decision proved to be a good one. As the situation in Europe heated up toward the end of the 1930s, Getty's politics fell more and more into disfavor. From 1937 to 1939, he traveled extensively in Germany and witnessed the beginnings of the persecutions that would eventually infect almost all of Europe.

The threat of war also offered a number of financial opportunities that Getty could simply not pass up. During his visit to Vienna in October 1938, he paid a visit to the home of the Austrian branch of the great banking family, the Rothschilds. Since the Nazi invasion, or *Anschluss,* the previous March, Baron Louis de Rothschild had been held prisoner while ransom negotiations were conducted with Hermann Goering, the highest-ranking Nazi officer after

The Pierre Hotel, New York City. Getty bought the building in 1938 for $2.35 million—less than a quarter of its original price.

Hitler. Rothschild's palace had been looted of his French eighteenth-century furniture, tapestries, silver, and paintings. When Getty inquired about when the furniture would be sold, he was told an auction would be held in January and that he would be informed later of the details.

Later, on November 10, 1938, known in Germany as *Kristallnacht* (the "night of glass," when thousands of Jewish shops and businesses were destroyed, along with the owners and their families), Getty was in New York pondering the sale of the Rothschild collection. He decided to bid $72,000 for two exquisite desks and was content to get them for $128,000 below their value of eight years previous. For Getty the war in Europe appeared to be a lucky development, one that offered him a fine opportunity to exploit the circumstances and come up with some truly memorable bargains.

Chapter 8

Getty
Does His Part

"The trouble is that everybody talks about how much money I make. I wonder what sort of accomplishment it is to make a lot of money?"
—*J. Paul Getty, interviewed in* Time *magazine*

Getty and Teddy Lynch were married in 1939, though they did not live together. She stayed in Rome to pursue her operatic career while he traveled to various destinations pursuing his two passions—money and women.

One of Getty's more lasting affairs was with a German woman named Hilde Kruger, a mysterious woman he met at a party given by Nazi leaders. Kruger was known in certain circles as "Hitler's girlfriend" and was not exactly an asset to Getty when he came under FBI scrutiny for possible espionage. Not only was his hotel, the Pierre, believed to be a hotbed of Nazi sympathizers and spies, but his public support and admiration for individuals such as Goebbels, Goering, and even Hitler himself cast him in an undeniably suspicious light. Through it all, Getty had also been trying to sell oil to the Nazis during his visits to Germany. Also, while Roosevelt was trying to win financial support from Great Britain, Getty invested heavily in the German government by buying bonds.

Unaware that he was under investigation, Getty tried once again to obtain a post in the Roosevelt administration. Finally, a friend informed him that the FBI had pictures of him with Hitler and that the press had been tailing Hilde Kruger, who was suspected of being a Nazi spy. This knowledge effectively ended Getty's pursuit of any governmental position.

After the Japanese surprise attack on Pearl Harbor in 1941, the United States entered World War II. Immediately after the attack, J. Edgar Hoover, the director of the FBI, personally issued approval for the arrest of J. Paul Getty as a possible enemy of America, though Getty was not to be brought in immediately. The delay in Getty's arrest was timely, for Sarah, now eighty-nine years old, came down with pneumonia the day after Christmas in 1941 and died. Getty was fairly shaken by the loss of his mother and, for a few days, grieved more openly than ever before. Sarah Getty was J. Paul's last real emotional tie in the world and without her, as he said, he felt "like an orphan."

The instructions in Sarah's will were clear—anyone who contested it would be treated as if "they never existed." Substantial sums were left to each of her four grandsons: George II inherited her mansion, Ronald received $200,000, and Paul, Jr., and Gordon each received $50,000. The rest of the money in the Sarah Getty Trust, the will stipulated, would be dispersed to the next generations of Gettys.

The close of 1941 was a terrible time for Getty. He had not only lost his mother, but Teddy had been arrested by Mussolini's police in Italy for being an American spy. In America, Getty could not seem to shake his unsavory reputation as a "pro-Nazi sympathizer." The growing distrust he felt from various business people and government officials made him a bit uneasy.

Perhaps, after he bought a controlling interest in the parent company, Getty chose his new position as president of Spartan Aircraft of Tulsa in an effort to change his reputation. Owned by Bill Skelly and Skelly Oil, Spartan produced aircraft for the war effort. Getty arrived to oversee production and to give his special boost to a slightly lagging operation.

As president of Spartan, Getty had a four-room blockhouse built for him. Right in the main flight path of a Tulsa airport, this protective shelter had twelve-inch walls above ground and eighteen-inch walls below. Constructed of concrete and steel, his new home was meant to provide safety from his greatest fears: the direct crash of a loaded bomber, the vicious tornadoes of the Midwest, and possible German *Luftwaffe* (air force) bombings.

Getty ousted Spartan's president-owner Bill Skelly from the top post at the company and immediately went to work on improving efficiency and quality. Getty had become obsessed with working for the war effort and devoted all his time to manag-

Louise (Teddie) Lynch, Getty's fifth wife, with their son Timmy, who died at age 12.

ing and overseeing the company. Working for the American cause seemed to bring out the most benevolent and selfless side of him. He became a dedicated factory manager, engineered machines, and dealt personally with all personnel matters. He stayed in the factory through the night on some occasions, rarely ate lunch, and paid himself $100 in nickels, which he would use for the soda machine. He even asked his employees to work without pay one Sunday in order to make a free trainer aircraft for the Navy. This idea was a terrific public relations move for Spartan as well as a great morale booster for its people.

The efficiency Getty was able to attain at the Spartan factory was quite remarkable, as was his ability to dedicate himself to mastering so many skills in such a short period of time. Most remarkable was that for the first time in his life, his efforts were poured wholeheartedly into a venture that was never meant to turn a penny in profit.

When the war ended, Getty worked to convert Spartan into a commercial producer of peacetime products. He explored the possibilities of manufacturing home appliances, refrigerators, and even cars. The final decision was to produce motor homes, and Getty approached that endeavor with the same enthusiasm he had brought to the war effort. He became fanatical about researching the smallest details and studying every bit of available information that would help to increase his chances of success. But Spartan motor homes did not succeed. As the company lost money, Getty lost interest.

In the meantime, Teddy had made her way safely back to America and, by 1946, had given birth prematurely to Getty's fifth son, Timmy, in California. Getty asked his secretary to send roses and something for the baby, "maybe a little hat." It wasn't until three weeks later that Getty traveled from Tulsa to Los Angeles to see Teddy and his fifth son in the hospital.

Chapter 9

The Getty Gamble

"I think having your own money in the business you are running makes you a lot sharper. Stockholders in my company at least have the consolation of knowing that if they lost money, I will lose a lot more."
—*J. Paul Getty*

*A*t the age of fifty-five in 1947, J. Paul Getty was no longer the lean, young lad who had come to Tulsa to make his fortune. His characteristic vanity increased to a point where he commissioned his second face-lift (his first was in 1939, at the age of forty-seven) and began to dye his hair. It was rumored that he even began ingesting sulphur in order to keep his hair a youthful red.

It was also a time when Getty began to speak about the one ambition he had other than business success: he yearned to be a beachcomber. After decades of dealing with the immense pressure of running a financial empire, and the stress from his many personal entanglements that had ended in scandal, he was ready to be free from all responsibilities. He was more than willing, as he said, to leave the day-to-day routines of the various corporations in the hands of the career executives.

*

*In court, George
essentially
brought action
challenging his
father's right to
retire.*

To achieve his goal, Getty began to consider selling off some of his company's holdings. At one point, he even considered selling all of Getty Oil to the Sunray Corporation for cash. Instead, he decided to concentrate on consolidating the Getty holdings, to sell off some Getty Oil stocks from the Sarah Getty Trust, to merge certain interests, and to simplify the structure of his empire.

Unfortunately for him, a number of concerned parties strongly opposed his plans. One of those opponents was Getty's eldest son, George II, then the co-trustee (with Thomas Dockweiler) of the Sarah Getty Trust. George argued that his father was trying to sell out for less than the true value of the shares he controlled. In court, he essentially brought action challenging his father's right to retire. J. Paul, who never took kindly to being challenged, fought back with a vengeance. He argued that the Sarah Getty Trust had been in incompetent hands since he left his post as trustee and that he should be reinstated as the sole director. The elder Getty won his case and, in 1948, was actively back in the oil business as sole trustee of the trust. Sunray, put off by the conflict surrounding the company, had lost all interest in buying Getty Oil. It seemed that Getty's beachcombing fantasy would be postponed indefinitely.

Frustrated by his thwarted attempt at retirement, Getty set his mind to expanding his corporate kingdom with more enthusiasm than he ever had before. He saw highways being constructed all across the country, the economy booming, and floods of automobiles in every town from coast to coast. He was convinced that soon America would not be able to meet all its oil needs independently and that other parts of the world would soon have to provide crude oil to satisfy America's enormous demand.

With international expansion in mind, Getty decided to pursue oil properties in the Middle East. He had already learned from various geologists and reports commissioned by the Truman administration that the Middle East and the Persian Gulf contained the world's vastest undiscovered oil reserves.

Before Getty decided to join the scene, the Mideast oil business was dominated by a group of seven companies known as the Seven Sisters. The group comprised British Petroleum, Royal Dutch-Shell, Standard Oil of New Jersey, Standard Oil of California, Socony Vacuum (soon to be Mobil), Texaco, and Gulf. Together they controlled more than 80 percent of Persian Gulf production, and had done so, unchallenged, for some time. They were not inclined to allow a feisty California oilman to share in their profits.

Getty had his eye on a small parcel of desert land called the Neutral Zone, bounded on the north by Kuwait, the south by Saudi Arabia, and the east by the Persian Gulf. Inhabited only by nomadic Bedouin tribes, it was desolate land that had caused Kuwait and Saudi Arabia to fight for centuries. Their final solution was that no one would own it; it would be neutral. They did, however, share in the mineral rights and agreed that if one country wanted to exploit its oil reserves both would have to consent and both would share in the profits. If each country found a company to drill, they agreed, the one to find oil first would share the benefits with the other. In effect, Kuwait and Saudi Arabia would be partners in any event.

By the time Getty took an interest in the Neutral Zone, the Kuwaiti concession had already gone to Amnioil, a huge conglomerate of many smaller oil interests. However, the Saudi concession was still open and available, and J. Paul Getty was determined to win it. His fiercest competition came from Amnioil, which also wanted to win the Saudi oil-drilling rights and stake a 100 percent claim to the oil in the Neutral Zone.

Up against stiff competition from Amnioil, Getty had to move fast. Positive of the oil potential in the Neutral Zone, and determined not to lose in the Middle East for a second time, Getty offered King Abdul Aziz of Saudi Arabia an $8 million down payment for the Saudi concession *sight unseen.* It was a brave, and potentially reckless, move but one that made the Saudis take immediate notice. Negotiations went back and forth and Getty finally sealed the concession with an agreement to pay the Saudis $9.5 million in cash, up front, plus a minimum payment of $1 million even if no oil was ever found. Then came the real shocker. Getty also agreed to pay the Saudis 55 cents for each barrel he took out of the ground. This royalty rate was two thirds higher than the one paid by Amnioil to Kuwait and two-and-a-half-times higher than the rate paid by the Seven Sisters in other parts of the Middle East.

Paying the highest oil royalty in history was not in keeping with Getty's shrewd and thrifty character. But his competitive drive and his confidence in the long-term soundness of this investment allowed him to see the deal through. His formal guarantee of the concession came from the Saudis on December 31, 1948, but only after Getty had agreed to provide housing for the oil workers, schools for their children, formal training programs, and mosques for prayer. What he did not know was that before finalizing with Getty, King Abdul Aziz offered one last chance at the concession to Amnioil if they could match Getty's price. Amnioil declined, reasoning that paying more to the Saudis than they did to Kuwait would create great diplomatic problems. Getty and Amnioil would, instead, become the two partners for the Neutral Zone.

Much of Getty's success in the Middle East was due to his unique business situation. As the sole decision-maker and principal member of Getty Oil, he could move fast, make deals, and not have to answer to anyone but himself. This offered him an incredible advantage over other large companies that could spend weeks in committee deliberating.

Together, Getty and Ralph E. Davies, head of Amnioil, planned their exploitation of the Neutral Zone. For some reason both oilmen developed, almost from the start, a distinct hatred for each other. They had heated arguments about drilling strategies and expenditures, for Getty wanted to keep the overhead of the operation extremely low to compensate for the high royalties he would be paying.

In the months and years that followed, Getty would not step foot in the Middle East. Instead, he sent George II to represent the Getty interests and to deal with Davies and Amnioil. For a long time after the drilling began, no oil was found and both companies began to doubt whether they should continue their efforts. Even J. Paul Getty became temporarily unsure of his business acumen and began to believe that this time he had failed on a grand scale. By 1952 no substantial oil had been tapped, tensions grew worse, and by 1953 the rift between the two partner companies reached its height. J. Paul Getty and Ralph Davies even refused to speak with each other.

Finally, on February 10, 1953, after four years of frustration and $30 million spent, a major oil strike was made in the Wafra region. The supply they found tapped into the Burghan oil field, one of the largest in the region. The strike was considered by many, including *Fortune* magazine, to be "somewhere between colossal and history-making."

When news of the strike became public, it took Getty Oil less than a month to double the price of its stock. Once again the master's gamble had turned into a full-blown jackpot.

Getty in 1960, at the launching of the tanker J. Paul Getty *in Le Havre, France.*

The Richest Man in the World

"He is the worst man I
have ever known."
—*A Wall Street broker*
speaking of J. Paul Getty

*T*he next eight years of
Getty's life, from 1951 to 1959, contained many highs
and lows. He spent much of this time traveling as a
nomad through Europe. Without his current wife
and child, he was able to travel with two or three
women at once and free to search the continent for
new art pieces, and new women, to add to his
respective collections.

Getty seemed oblivious to the connections and
responsibilities he had contracted in the past. Back in
the United States, for instance, young Timmy was in
poor health. He had suffered from eye trouble at
birth, and at age six he developed a tumor the size of
an egg between his eyes. The tumor severely
affected his eyesight and required several operations. Timmy's father was ten thousand miles away.

While visiting a London art gallery, Getty was
introduced to Penelope Kitson, a slender beauty

who enchanted the oilman as soon as he saw her. Penelope was unhappily married and was easily lured away from her husband to a position as Getty's personal assistant and adviser. She would remain his companion for the rest of his life.

Meanwhile, Timmy was undergoing painful brain surgery in Los Angeles to remove another tumor that was pressing on his optic nerve and causing him to become blind. In touch with Getty throughout the ordeal, Teddy urged him to visit his family. But he would always profess to have an extremely important business deal pending that made such a visit impossible. Instead, he would complain of Timmy's costly hospital bills.

Against all the odds, Timmy recovered from his second series of operations. After a four-year separation, Teddy took her son to Europe to visit his father. During this visit, Teddy became aware of Penelope's relationship with J. Paul and realized that their marriage was completely finished. Teddy had hoped her husband would return with her to the United States, but he refused. Instead, he asked her to stay in Europe and promised to make her "as rich as Queen Elizabeth." Teddy refused.

In 1956 Teddy filed for divorce in Los Angeles. The next year, Timmy's tumor reappeared and necessitated three more terrible operations. By May 1958 the divorce papers came through and Timmy seemed cured, though he was blind and his head was misshapen. Unfortunately, he died in August 1958 while under anesthetic for a final operation to reset the bones in his skull that had been disfigured by the tumors. Teddy, who had no one else, was destroyed by the loss of her only child. Moreover, in typical Getty fashion, she was left by herself to pay the hospital bills and to make all the arrangements for the funeral.

If Getty felt any real emotion at the loss of the son he professed to have loved more than the others, no one really knew. Getty always felt that emotion

was a weakness and a vulnerability to which he would not allow himself to fall prey. He was not present at Timmy's funeral and gave his pressing negotiations for an Italian refinery as an excuse for not attending.

Getty with Robina Lund, his lawyer and one of his many female companions.

Even with his various personal tragedies, Getty managed to concentrate on business, and by the end of the 1950s he was considered by most to be the richest man in the world.

Greater dreams of expansion caused Getty to invest $200 million in a new East Coast refinery in Delaware, an operation he hoped to utilize for turning crude oil into gasoline for automobiles. He also spent $60 million to improve his Avon refinery in California, doubled the number of Tide Water gas stations across the country, and spent $207 million to build special supertankers that transported his crude oil to Europe, America, and Japan. By the time Getty was finished expanding, Tide Water ranked seventh in its share of the total United States gasoline market. Getty had achieved his goal in the Middle East. He was a key player and on a par with the Seven Sisters.

Getty's secret to success was the crude "garbage" oil he took out of the shallow sands of the Neutral Zone. His low overhead (he never carried more than seven hundred employees) and the relative ease with which the "garbage" oil came out of the ground enabled Getty to sell his crude for a very attractive price without sacrificing a healthy profit.

The first decade Getty Oil became established in the Middle East, from 1948 to 1957, saw Getty's worth escalate from $80 million to more than $300 million. The Sarah Getty Trust was then valued at $200 million, more than seventy times what it had been worth in 1934 when it was created. On paper, Getty was worth even more than that. With his various other holdings, such as the Pierre Hotel, Spartan Aircraft, his art collection, and sundry other assets, *Fortune* magazine declared him the richest man in America at the age of sixty-five, worth almost $1 billion.

This announcement brought Getty almost instant celebrity, and with it, a life much more in the public view. The notoriety did not upset him, for he liked publicity and power; he was simply unprepared for the instant attention he unexpectedly began to receive. Reporters and photographers began to follow him everywhere. He told one reporter, "I can't say it thrills me. When one is very rich it doesn't especially matter to be just a bit richer than someone else. I've never really been able to count mine."

The Richest Man in the World

But, in addition to his legendary cheapness, J. Paul Getty was known as a man who did not enjoy his money at all. One close friend said, "I don't believe for a moment that he gets any enjoyment out of his money. He's a miser—period." Others constantly accused him, as Oscar Wilde once put it, of being a "man who knew the price of everything and the value of nothing." Now, whether he enjoyed it or not, the entire world knew of his wealth and wanted nothing more than to sit back and watch what a man with so much money could really do.

Getty at Sutton Place, prior to his purchase of the estate in 1959.

Chapter *11*

The Fortune
and the Fame

"I don't know of
anybody who could sell
out for more than I
could."
—*J. Paul Getty*

J. Paul Getty greeted the worldwide publicity about his wealth with mixed feelings. On one hand, the publicity meant he was finally acknowledged as both a powerful business leader and a financial genius. This sort of acclaim was not something he was unhappy to receive. But it also meant that now the entire world was watching. And the world knew that Getty had more money than anyone else. Photographers and reporters covered his every move relentlessly, leaving him with little or none of the anonymity he came to cherish.

International renown also made Getty paranoid. He began to fear kidnappers and extortionists, as well as those who would be spying on him to learn his secrets. He also dreaded the thousands of people who would write, call, or hound him in person for a chance at a charitable donation or a simple handout.

While on his next trip to England in 1959, Getty stumbled upon an opportunity that helped him solve much of the publicity dilemma he faced. He was taken by a friend, Louis Weiller, to a party at Sutton Place, owned by the Duke of Sutherland in Guildford, Surrey. In England at that time, taxes were very heavy and many of Britain's nobility and landed gentry were hard-pressed to keep their family fortunes intact. Many great estates, coming up against economic hard times and large tax debts, were eagerly sold to buyers with ready cash.

The Duke of Sutherland had bought Sutton Place in 1917 for 120,000 pounds sterling (about $600,000). By 1959, however, his many family farms were overstaffed and he needed cash in a hurry. Getty, the uncanny bargain-sniffer, decided to pursue the idea of obtaining Sutton Place "for a song." He offered the duke 50,000 pounds (about $140,000) for the house and about 60 acres of land. His friend Louis Weiller was embarrassed that Getty had offered such a low price (it didn't even cover the cost of the estate's two swimming pools). Unbelievably, however, the duke accepted Getty's offer, although the exact amount finally agreed upon is a matter of great dispute. Getty later estimated that he had acquired the estate at better than one-twentieth of its replacement value and judged it to be one of the best deals he had ever made.

Sutton Place was, in its own right, a notable structure of historical as well as architectural significance. Built in the sixteenth century, it was once owned by King Henry VIII, and had been given by the king to one of his favorite courtiers, Sir Richard Weston. Several of King Henry's wives had stayed at Sutton Place, and it was said that Weston's son Francis was beheaded for allegedly seducing Anne Boleyn on the grounds one evening. Getty's bed, in the master bedroom, gave him an added thrill because it was one of the beds that King Henry slept in while married to Anne Boleyn.

Architecturally, too, Sutton Place was impressive. Its exterior, an imposing facade of stone, brick, and stained glass, was almost intimidating in its grandeur. Many people who knew Getty found an ironic similarity between the cold rigidity of the mansion's stone and the coldness of its owner. Sutton Place contained more than a dozen reception rooms, including the Long Gallery, which measured 165 feet in length and was said to be the largest hall in Britain. The 70-foot dining table, bought from newspaper magnate William Randolph Hearst, could seat 100 guests, a good many of whom could stay the night in the 14 stately bedrooms.

This was, for all intents and purposes, Getty's first private and permanent residence. It soon became the official European headquarters of Getty Oil, as well as a place for his ever-growing collection of art and antiques. Most of all, Getty enjoyed his new home because, among other things, it was much cheaper to live there than to stay in hotels. Chatting with his friend Art Buchwald one night, Getty informed him that their drinks, Buchwald's tomato juice and Getty's rum and Coke, would cost one dollar at his old residence, the Ritz. Then, obviously pleased, he figured that their drinks only cost a dime at Sutton Place. He went on to calculate that dinner at home would cost $2.50 a person, whereas a similar dinner at Maxim's would easily be $10 a head.

The official opening of Getty's estate was an elaborate affair that also served as the coming-out party of Jeannette Constable-Maxwell, the daughter of Getty's English investor and friend Ian Constable-Maxwell. Costs for the party ran more than $30,000 and were split by the two hosts. Despite the fact that the party set Getty back about $15,000, he seemed to enjoy himself. As the night wore on, he was heard to say, "I'm going to dance as long as there are any pretty girls to dance with."

An article in *Newsweek* covered the occasion and pointed out that, during the twelve hours in which

Most of all, Getty enjoyed his new home because, among other things, it was much cheaper to live there than to stay in hotels.

Getty bought Sutton Place in 1959 from the Duke of Sutherland "for a song." Above, an exterior view; above right, the dining room; and below right, the library.

Von Bulow moved into Sutton Place and was enlisted mainly to "amuse Getty at meals."

the party took place, Getty's oil interests alone earned him about $57,000. That means Getty came out at the end of the evening richer than he was at the beginning.

The three hundred dinner guests were served stuffed peacock and boar's head as well as caviar and hot dogs. Drinks included a variety of champagnes worth more than $10,000. One of the party's more unusual touches was the free-roaming Guernsey cow called Jessie, provided by the Milk Marketing Board, which also sponsored a milk bar offering nonalcoholic drinks to the guests. Jessie was the brainstorm of one of Getty's new aides, Claus von Bulow, who organized most of the party. Von Bulow, a tall, regal Danish lawyer, took an instant liking to Getty and was quickly accepted as a member of his inner circle. As a personal aide, Von Bulow moved into Sutton Place and was enlisted mainly to "amuse Getty at meals." Apparently, he did his job well because he remained a friend for the rest of Getty's life.

Jeannette Constable-Maxwell, however, was not the only person to make her debut that evening. It was, in fact, the first time Getty had been introduced to England's nobility and the first time he was accorded the respect and recognition due a man of his stature and influence. But all his money and power could not make him the urbane sophisticate he fancied himself to be. He was still a simple oilman from the Midwest who, though he liked to flaunt his Oxford degree, spent most of his life concerned with little more than making money.

One of Getty's biggest social *faux pas*, and probably the one for which he is most famous (or infamous), was his installation of a pay phone for guests at Sutton Place. It was, quite simply, a coinbox telephone identical to those found in public places all over England, with a sign above it that read "Public Telephone." He did it because he believed guests and workmen were constantly picking up the phones and calling long distances. A call from Sutton Place to London cost about eighteen cents but, as Getty put it, "when you get some fellow talking for ten or fifteen minutes, well, it adds up." Getty often liked to recall the fact that William Randolph Hearst had once expelled a guest from San Simeon (Hearst's mansion) for making a phone call without his permission. Embarrassing publicity about the famous pay phone soon grew too much and Getty finally surrendered. He moved it downstairs to the cloakroom where it would hardly ever be used.

Getty's legendary cheapness was the source of much debate among the people who knew him. Some were convinced it was just an act devised to keep others from taking advantage of him. But he did not want the world to think of him as a miser. And one friend went so far as to say that he was "generous as long as nobody knew about it."

It seems, though, that the majority of people did not "know about it." What they saw was an unyielding face caught in a permanent scowl—a man who appeared almost never to enjoy himself or the others around him. Most everyone was treated with an evenhanded coolness that rarely ever changed.

Getty did seem to enjoy tending to the smallest details of everyday life, particularly if those details involved money. He sat one day to figure out what his gatekeeper's salary should be. He did this by multiplying the number of times per day that the gate was opened by a fixed dollar amount. His calculations revealed that his gatekeeper was worth $5.60 a week, and that is what he was paid. He used similar methods of calculation in his art collecting as well. Often he would figure what to bid on an oil painting by assigning a monetary value to each square inch of the piece, measuring its full dimensions and then multiplying.

Other eccentricities surfaced as Getty got older and subsequently richer. His fear for his own safety and his preoccupation with his health grew worse in later years. He refused to fly anywhere, and he was very superstitious about sailing (perhaps because of that trip on the *Lusitania* shortly before it was torpedoed). He also became obsessed with his own physical prowess, lifting weights well into his seventies, and taking a number of treatments and medications in an effort to delay his inevitable aging. His bathroom was filled with pills, bottles, ointments, and prescriptions in enormous quantities. Fearing the loss of a business deal due to illness, he would become violently upset if he were exposed to a person with so much as a cold.

His preoccupation with women, particularly young women, was no secret either. Known as quite an exceptional lover, Getty was constantly reaffirming his virility and masculinity. He felt that success with women and success in business were very much related and believed that his business success pushed his romantic drive, and vice versa. As he grew older, he felt his injections of H-3, a serum taken to dull his various aches and pains, gave him renewed sexual energy. He also thought his anti-tremor medication increased his sexual prowess and, even after his tremors decreased, he continued taking the medicine.

Perhaps much of this strange and obsessive behavior was the inevitable result of an aging man who had led a life of intense pressure and responsibility. Or maybe Getty's more sedentary life style at Sutton Place, sheltered and mostly alone, caused him to withdraw more and more into himself. Whatever the reason, Getty had reached the point where he would not walk the grounds of his estate without the escort of his trained German Shepherd attack dogs and an armed guard who followed him close behind, on the lookout for any threat of danger.

Chapter *12*

Family Affairs

"I'm a bad boss. A good boss develops successors. There is nobody to step into my shoes."
—*J. Paul Getty*

As an oilman, Getty was unlike anyone who had come before him. He owned 80 percent of Getty Oil Company, more than any single owner of any major company in the world. Getty Oil executives in Los Angeles were forced to contend with a boss who was thousands of miles away, removed from the daily grind of corporate life, yet still completely in control. J. Paul Getty remained involved in every detail of the company's operation— from the biggest multi-million-dollar investment to reducing the cost of flushing the workers' toilets in the Neutral Zone. No one in Los Angeles was to make any moves without consulting him first.

Not only was business tough for Getty's California people to conduct, but they were not well paid either. Getty believed in a simple day's wage for a good day's work. Consequently, he did not offer any pensions, benefits, or stock-option programs to his employees. By oil industry standards, Getty Oil lagged far behind its competitors in employee compensation and had a reputation for perpetuating dull, plodding bureaucrats who had little imagination or drive.

By the late 1950s, Getty was ready to try another great expansion scheme. He invested $600 million to improve and enlarge many of his American refineries, tankers, and gas stations, and spent an additional $200 million building a state-of-the-art refinery in Delaware. He was determined to become the "eighth sister" of the Middle East oil world.

Getty began by flooding the American market with Middle East "garbage" oil, which was both cheap and easy to produce. As expected, many of America's oil producers in Texas, Oklahoma, Louisiana, and California became quite annoyed by Getty's actions and began to apply pressure on the Eisenhower administration in Washington, D.C., to do something about it. In 1957 Eisenhower instituted a voluntary import quota system that was meant to protect domestic oil concerns. The new quota allowed so little Getty oil to enter the United States that, if complied with, the Delaware refinery would be rendered almost useless. Getty, or someone powerful in his organization, decided to disobey the Eisenhower quota system and, since it was technically voluntary, no laws were being broken. But other producers took their lead from Getty, and Eisenhower saw that the quotas were not working. After deliberation, Eisenhower issued a presidential proclamation that made the quota system mandatory and effectively stopped Getty's grand plan for importing massive quantities of Mideast oil to the United States. It also meant, however, that the economy would have to rely more heavily on expensive domestic oil, raising the cost of production in many industries and ultimately weakening the economy.

And so Getty's expansion plan turned out to be an $800 million mistake. At the same time, price wars in California caused Tide Water to lose some of its market share which, in turn, started to create other losses. Getty now felt it was an opportune time for him to pare down his business and to minimize his debt.

Although Getty had four children, none of them were ever groomed to inherit the family business. Their father had never spent any time with them and had never taught them any of the ins and outs of a complicated and difficult industry. As a result, they remained mostly ignorant about the oil trade throughout their adult lives.

Observers close to the family said Getty was often a cruel father who didn't seem to care about helping his children to succeed. Paul, Jr., remembered an occasion in high school when he had written his father a letter in an attempt to make some contact. Getty responded by correcting the grammar and spelling, and returning it without a message.

Even without a normal relationship, Getty's sons each felt the need to prove themselves to their father and to try to learn to take on the responsibilities that were their birthright. What made their attempts even more difficult was the fact that there was little affection between the brothers themselves, nothing of a shared life or experience, and no support and guidance from each other as compensation for lacking a father. Instead, each was left to contend alone with the overwhelming demands of Getty Oil and the lone tyrant who ran it.

George II, Getty's oldest son, showed the most business promise of the four and was the son who spent the most time involved in the workings of Getty Oil. At thirty-six, George was president of Tidewater (which had changed its name to the single word when Getty gained control) and seemed to be the logical heir apparent to his father's kingdom. Unfortunately, however, George did not have the temperament to step into his father's shoes. Having been repeatedly intimidated and humiliated by his

Getty's relationship with his sons was troubled. Shown here (clockwise from above) are Gordon (born 1933), George (born 1924, pictured with fiancée Barbara Lyon), Ronald (born 1929), and Jean Paul Jr. (born 1932).

father, George developed a profound sense of insecurity about himself and his business acumen. Still, he tried fiercely to please his father and, though he was considered to be plodding and somewhat uninteresting, he did manage to cultivate a sense of fair play and civic responsibility that J. Paul Getty never had.

A battle over the sale of Tidewater brought father and son head-to-head in their first and only real battle. Some of the company's western marketing properties were losing money and George wanted to sell them to Standard Oil for $300 million. The deal was soon stopped by an antitrust arm of the Justice Department that claimed the sale would be a serious violation on a number of counts. J. Paul Getty was quick to strike out at his son, making it clear that he felt George had failed as Tidewater's president. Wresting control of the deal, Paul arranged to sell the western properties to Phillips Petroleum (a subsidiary of Amnioil) for $309 million. Before the deal could go through, however, there was another battle with the Justice Department. This time, J. Paul Getty emerged victorious and had completed the largest sale of his career. George remained humiliated both by the fact that the sale was completed without him and that it brought Getty Oil $9 million more than he had originally anticipated.

Getty's other three sons—Ronald (the son of Fini, the third wife), Paul, Jr., and Gordon (the sons of Ann, the fourth wife)—all tried their hand in the oil business at various times. Each son inevitably failed due to lack of experience, and each was eventually fired by executives from various arms of the organization. Getty's sons had hoped to establish some connection with their estranged father by taking part in his empire. Instead, they became serious financial liabilities and their failings created a wider rift between their father and themselves. Paul, Jr., who had always shown a flair for art, could never bring himself to care very much about making money. As a result, his attempted contribution to the family business was a complete failure. Gordon, who cultivated a love of classical-music composition, was equally ill-suited to corporate life. Ronald, the second oldest, who had been a discipline problem from an early age, would not enter into the world of business until after his father was dead.

The next major conflict between father and son was initiated by Gordon in the mid-1960s. Not interested in a career in business, Gordon decided to demand that Getty Oil shares start paying a cash dividend, ensuring him of an annual income. His father, who was never one to be given directives, was outraged at his son's arrogance. After refusing to consider the request, J. Paul suddenly found himself threatened with a lawsuit by his youngest child. Hoping to avoid the hassles of litigation, and the bad publicity that accompanied it, Getty decided to comply with his son's wishes and pay Gordon an annual dividend on his shares from the Sarah Getty Trust.

A few years later, however, Gordon decided that his income was insufficient. He then demanded that the shares be declared at a higher value and initiated a series of fights to achieve that goal. These battles were not to be solved quickly and they plagued the elder Getty for many years to come. At the center of these conflicts was Gordon's claim that his father denied the purpose of the trust by not fairly distributing the wealth from its dividends to its beneficiaries. Numerous and lengthy court battles followed and Gordon, now a *persona non grata*, was entirely written out of his father's will.

Gordon's lawsuit was finally lost on a technicality when J. Paul's lawyers produced a document of mysterious origin. Somehow a rider had been attached to the Sarah Getty Trust that gave complete control of the holding to J. Paul Getty. This clearly went against Sarah's intentions, which were not only to protect her grandchildren from their father's possible recklessness, but also to provide incomes for her heirs. It appeared that, somehow, Paul had tricked his mother, deaf and sick on her deathbed, into signing a typewritten rider that overruled the provisions she had earlier set forth. Without this piece of paper, Gordon would have won his case.

The scandal surrounding Gordon's lawsuit was soon overshadowed by three tragedies that struck the Getty family in the early 1970s. The first involved Talitha Pol, the wife of Paul, Jr. Talitha shared her husband's love of wild parties, heavy drinking, drugs, and other forms of self-destructive behavior that characterized most of the time they spent together in Rome. Paul, Jr.'s excessive womanizing was partly to blame for the marital problems they began to experience in 1971. After a few months, and a number of failed reconciliations, Talitha was found by the police in her apartment after taking a massive overdose of heroin, which proved to be fatal.

George II was also a deeply troubled man. Though he had gained minor prominence in the Getty empire, and was a well-respected business leader in California, he was never able to rid himself of the overwhelming sense of failure he felt in himself. His father, who never offered any sense of approval, had made him feel unloved and frequently humiliated him in front of other top Getty executives. As a consequence, in the early 1970s, George became obsessed by a desire to win approval for what he had accomplished. The result was that certain aspects of his personal life began to fall apart. First, his marriage of sixteen years disintegrated due to what his wife, Gloria Gordon, called his "cold indifference." Following a subsequent marriage to multimillionaire Jackie Riordan, his life did not improve. His second marriage quickly floundered as George began to drink heavily and to take various medications to help him sleep. As time went on, he also became exceptionally irritable and moody.

On the night of June 5, 1973, George drank several beers and an entire bottle of wine before he appeared on the balcony of his home with a gun. After firing a shot into the air, he ran into the kitchen, grabbed a barbecue knife, and began to shout at his wife that he was going to kill himself. He then drew the knife across his abdomen, making a superficial wound that was just deep enough to draw blood. As Jackie called the company doctor, George raved about being "strong, powerful, and able to bear pain." By 12:30 a.m. on June 6, the police arrived to find George had locked himself in his bedroom with a gun and had taken a lethal dose of pills. He died hours later, after finally passing out and being rushed to the hospital by police. The Los Angeles coroner later found multiple bruises and lacerations on George's body, evidently caused by self-inflicted mutilation with a letter opener and other objects.

For many who knew George, there was no doubt that his anguish stemmed from his feelings of hatred and frustration toward his father. Five days before his death he had written a will that left $10,000 to J. Paul Getty, a final act of both confusion and anger. George had shown a similar sense of hopelessness in the past when, on his father's birthday and on Christmas, he sent his father a check for $100. These actions, and those that followed, were a testament to the pathetic lack of love and understanding that existed between the elder Getty and his children.

When news of George's death reached Sutton Place, J. Paul Getty sat and stared dumbly into space for half an hour, refusing to talk to or acknowledge anyone. Then his mourning period was suddenly over and he cooly set himself to planning who would replace George in the company.

Only five weeks later, another tragedy struck the Getty family. On July 10, 1973, Paul III (son of Paul, Jr., and his first wife, Gail) was kidnapped while walking down a secluded street in Rome. When the news hit the media, there was immediate speculation about the authenticity of the kidnap-

ping. Some believed it was simply a stunt staged to extort money from the richest man in the world. But Paul, Jr., and his ex-wife Gail were convinced that their son was in terrible danger. After initial demands by the kidnappers for approximately $1 million were rebuffed by the Gettys, the kidnappers' threats became increasingly more serious. They began to threaten mutilation of Paul III if their ransom demands were not quickly met. J. Paul Getty, however, remained convinced that the entire story was a hoax, engineered only to deprive him of some of his millions.

On November 10, a package arrived at the Italian newspaper *Il Messagero*. In it was a human ear and a lock of Paul III's reddish hair, which was

Getty's grandson, Paul III, after his release from kidnappers who cut off his right ear when Getty refused to meet their demands.

quickly identified by his mother as authentic. A note now demanded $3.2 million and threatened to send the rest of Paul III "cut into little pieces" if the money was not swiftly forthcoming. This development, however, did not immediately convince J. Paul Getty to give in to the kidnapper's demands. The rest of the family then made a formal offer of $1 million, which the kidnappers quickly rejected. Finally, unable to bear the thought of his seventeen-year-old grandson's further mutilation, the elder Getty gave in and engineered the delivery of $3.2 million to the kidnappers.

Paul III was released on December 15, his grandfather's eighty-first birthday. On that day, J. Paul Getty let it be known that his grandson's freedom was the greatest birthday present he could have received. Out of the total amount of ransom paid, only $17,000 was ever recovered, and many of the individuals responsible were never apprehended. The kidnapping of Paul III amounted to the greatest, and perhaps the *only,* swindle of J. Paul Getty ever recorded.

A Leap Toward Immortality

*B*y the mid-1970s, the Getty Oil fortune had grown so large that it was fairly self-perpetuating. Its owner bothered himself less and less with the mundane details of running the organization and focused his energy on his art collecting. He had studied at great length, and, in addition to acquiring a substantial collection, had even written a book on the subject.

It seems that part of Getty's desire to collect stemmed from his need to feel that, with all his money, he had acquired a certain sense of taste. But, in most cases, the way in which he went about collecting displayed very little, if any, real class. In almost every case, Getty was looking for a bargain first, and a work of art second. He almost never purchased anything that he felt was selling at its market value or higher. And the size of the objects he pursued was always important, as he felt that the

Getty, in an uncommonly frivolous gesture, dons a Beatles-style wig at a children's party in Surrey, England.

larger the piece, the more he was getting for his money. Much of his collection was frequently slighted by the critics, and Getty would forever regret that the art world never grew to take him very seriously.

His creation of an enormous art museum in Malibu, California, was perhaps partly an effort to finally demonstrate his commitment to the fine arts.

It was also, no doubt, his only option for leaving a legacy that would last long after he was gone.

Getty, with his life-long admiration for the great Roman emperors, had always loved the luxurious villas they had built during the imperial period. His particular favorite was the Villa dei Papyrii in Pompeii, which had been destroyed by the volcanic eruption of Mount Vesuvius in A.D. 79. Getty was determined to re-create the villa in Malibu and wanted it to serve as the permanent home of his art collection. But even with this professed love for the project, and the fact that he spent more than $17 million to complete it, he never once set foot on its grounds.

By the time the museum was ready to open to the public, Getty had managed to amass a fairly important collection of French furniture. His collection of antiques was considered to be the third most important in the world, dwarfed only by those in the Metropolitan Museum of Art in New York and the Museum of Fine Arts in Boston. His French furniture was, undoubtedly, the finest private collection in America. Getty also had sent all of his greatest pieces from Sutton Place to Malibu and had established the Getty Fine Arts Corporation to administer the business of the museum. In addition, he provided the museum with one of the largest endowments in history by leaving it the heir to the majority of his shares in Getty Oil. Though this act was surely a great one for the world of art, it was not done purely out of a new-found love for humanity. Later in his life, as his wealth multiplied, Getty used donations of his art as a means by which to offset paying substantial taxes on his income. In addition, he had already turned bitterly against each of his remaining sons for various reasons and was loathe to leave them any satisfaction upon his death.

J. Paul Getty's final years were typically marked by various disputes within the family and those who surrounded him at Sutton Place. During this period,

Margaret, Duchess of Argyll, guides Jean Paul's hand at his eightieth birthday party in 1972.

he rewrote his will a total of twenty-one times, on each instance adding or omitting whoever had gained or lost his favor at the time. Mostly, his last months were spent as a sad and lonely old man, secluded in his enormous mansion in Surrey. One of his final diary entries reveals his last regret to be the fact that he had forgotten the day his dog Shaun had died. This, and other complaints of shoulder pain, comprised his last recorded thoughts.

On June 6, 1976, three years to the day that his son George had taken his life, Jean Paul Getty died. Only a month earlier, he had been diagnosed as suffering from cancer. It is estimated that, upon his death, his personal wealth exceeded $2 billion dollars. The great billionaire, however, had died with only $16.41 in his pocket.

The Getty Museum in Malibu reflects his love of large, opulent art pieces.

Chapter *14*

The Legacy

"Mr. Getty is the
smartest businessman I
know. Coming to see
him is like a visit to
Mount Olympus."
—*George Getty II*

*A*ll in all, J. Paul Getty left four million shares in Getty Oil, worth more than $661 million, as a tax-free gift to his museum in Malibu. The eight million shares that the Sarah Getty Trust owned in Getty Oil, worth $1.3 billion, would not, however, go to his sons. Instead, the shares would skip a generation and would go to his sixteen grandchildren decades later. This avoided handing over the bulk of the Getty fortune in taxes to the government upon his death. The income from the shares in the trust, however, would go to Paul, Jr., Gordon, and George II's three daughters.

Various amounts of money, ranging from a few hundred dollars per year to $4,500 per month, were left to the sundry women companions and ex-wives Getty had left behind. Most of these women were severely disappointed when the will was actually read, many of them having been promised for years that they would be well provided for. A few of Getty's old companions even went so far as to file lawsuits to claim their right to a greater inheritance. Ronald was specifically bequeathed only $320,000 worth of stock, but as executor of the estate, he received $4.2 million. His brothers, however, would receive checks for more than $1.2 million every three months and would eventually be collecting more than $28 million per year.

The apportionment of Getty's estate continued to cause bitterness between his heirs for years. It managed, in some instances, to cause more hate and conflict between family members than ever existed before. In some ways this, more than the money, was the true legacy left by J. Paul Getty.

While it is true that most of the people who shared their lives with J. Paul Getty were plagued with unhappiness, it is also true that Getty himself was a fundamentally troubled man. In most cases, the coldness with which he treated his family was to be expected from a man who had received little affection from his own parents, as was his inability to form emotional ties of lasting value. In the end, what really mattered to J. Paul Getty was money, and he was ultimately willing to pay the price of success by spending both his life and his final days estranged from his family. That, it seems, was the one price J. Paul Getty never considered carefully enough.

Regardless of his personality and his apparent lack of friendliness, J. Paul Getty possessed the two traits essential to any great business person: talent and courage. His talent was the ability to see the bargain in almost any business situation—and to shrewdly negotiate terms that would take maximum advantage of an opponent's misfortune. His courage was his conviction to do it all himself. Getty consistently ignored the fact that his company was often bidding against corporations ten times his own size, and he refuted the idea that those corporations were automatically entitled to a market share just because they had been around longer.

Indeed, Getty's uniqueness, and some say the strength of Getty Oil, was the fact that he was personally and ultimately in charge of every aspect of his business. In the scope of the international oil trade, and other corporations with equal power and influence, Getty and his company were an amazing testament to the fact that one man *could* remain "at the helm" practically forever. Getty was somewhat driven by stubborness. Or perhaps he became convinced that no one else could meet his standards of competence. Whatever his logic, J. Paul Getty led a small family company from Tulsa, Oklahoma, into the global oil arena and made it a "key player"—one that helped to direct the course of international business.

Many would say that Getty's methods were not always sound, and many would say his brash management style and lack of personal warmth were severe handicaps, but he was, in the final analysis, a success. One could argue that in business that's all that really matters.

Bibliography

Davis, Douglas. "Welcome to Gettyland," *Newsweek*. January 28, 1974: p. 84.

Getty, J. Paul. *As I See It*. Englewood Cliffs, NJ: Prentice Hall, 1976.

Getty, J. Paul. *How to Be Rich*. New York: Berkeley Publishing Group, 1983.

Getty, J. Paul. *My Life and Fortunes*. California: Duell, Sloan & Pierce, 1963.

Hewins, Ralph. *The Richest American: J. Paul Getty*. New York: E. P. Dutton, 1960.

Lenzer, Robert. *The Life and Loves of J.P. Getty: The Richest Man in the World*. New York: Crown, 1986.

"The Do-It-Yourself Tycoon," *Time* (cover story). February 24, 1958: pp. 89-94.

"Quite Social, Eh?" *Newsweek*. July 11, 1960: p. 34.

Index

Acknowledgments and Credits

Frontispiece, pages 22–23, 28, 38–39, 42, 46–47, 50, 54, 58, 67, 74, 77, 84, 85 top, 85 bottom, 92, 97, 100, 102, Associated Press/ Wide World Photos.

Pages 10, 11 top, 11 bottom, 16, 18, 19, Crown Publishers, Inc.

Page 34, California Historical Society, Los Angeles History Center Photographic Collections.

Pages 52–53, 104, the J. Paul Getty Museum, Julius Schulman.

Page 60, Culver Pictures, Inc.

Page 63, courtesy the Pierre Hotel.

Page 80, Bettman Archives.